EVERYONE EATS™

EGGS

Jillian Powell

RSVP
RAINTREE
STECK-VAUGHN
PUBLISHERS
The Steck-Vaughn Company

Austin, Texas

Titles in the series

BREAD   EGGS   FISH   FRUIT   MILK
PASTA   POTATOES   RICE

Published by Raintree Steck-Vaughn Publishers,
an imprint of Steck-Vaughn Company
Everyone Eats™ is a trademark of Steck-Vaughn Company.

Library of Congress Cataloging-in-Publication Data
Powell, Jillian.
Eggs / Jillian Powell.
p.   cm.—(Everyone eats)
Includes bibliographical references and index.
Summary: Discusses different kinds of eggs, where they
come from, their nutritional value, and various ways to
prepare them. Includes several recipes.
ISBN 0-8172-4759-9
1. Eggs as food—Juvenile literature.
2. Cookery (Eggs)—Juvenile literature.
3. Eggs—Juvenile literature.
[1. Eggs.]
I. Title. II. Series: Powell, Jillian. Everyone Eats.
TX556.E4P69   1997
641.3'754—dc20   96-32830

Printed in Italy. Bound in the United States.
1 2 3 4 5 6 7 8 9 0 01 00 99 98 97

Picture acknowledgments

British Egg Information Service contents page, 17 (both), 18 (top), 19 (top); Bruce
Coleman 4 (bottom), 5 (top), 6, 8 (both), 13, 20, 25 (bottom), 23 (bottom), 24;
The Hutchison Library 12; Life File 4 (top), 5 (bottom), 7 (top), 18 (bottom), 19
(bottom), 21 (top), 22, 25 (top); Topham Picturepoint 7 (bottom), 23 (top);
Wayland Picture Library title page.

Contents

Extraordinary Eggs

Eggs are extraordinary. They range from the tiny eggs of fish and insects to huge alligator and ostrich eggs. All animal life comes from an egg, although many animals carry their eggs inside their bodies instead of laying them like birds and reptiles. A baby comes from an egg inside its mother's body. Dinosaurs laid eggs, and fossilized dinosaur eggs have been found, although for a long time no one knew what they were.

▲ Birds' eggs can be many different sizes. The largest egg in this picture is an ostrich egg, the smallest is a quail's egg. In the middle is a chicken's egg.

▶ A grass snake with her eggs. Snakes lay eggs but they also eat birds' eggs as part of their diet.

Ostrich chicks hatch from their shells while their parents guard the nest.

Birds are different shapes and sizes and so are their eggs. Ostrich eggs can be 8 inches long and weigh up to 4 pounds. The shell is so strong that a 275-pound weight could be placed on it without breaking it. An average ostrich egg would make an omelette to feed ten people! Compare that with the tiny egg laid by the vervain hummingbird of Jamaica. It is less than half an inch long and weighs as little as 0.0129 ounces.

These are the eggs of the lumpfish. They are a luxury food but are not as expensive as caviar from the sturgeon.

The eggs of many birds, fish, and even reptiles can be eaten. People eat eggs laid by ducks, geese, pigeons, gulls, turtles, ostriches, and even crocodiles. Some eggs are very expensive luxury foods, such as snails' eggs and the tiny black eggs of the sturgeon fish, which are called caviar. We also eat eggs from fish like salmon, lumpfish, and cod.

Eggs in the Past

Thousands of years ago, people found that some eggs were good to eat. At first they ate the eggs they found in the wild, probably raw or roasted in their shells over open fires. People may also have stored eggs during the winter months (when birds stopped laying) by burying them in ash. Then they learned how to keep the birds so that they could eat eggs every day.

The chickens we raise today are descended from the wild jungle birds of India. The practice of raising them spread from India to Africa, China, Japan, and parts of Europe about 4,000 years ago. Eggs were important in Ancient Greek and Roman cooking. The Romans had a custom of smashing the shells on their plates to prevent evil spirits from hiding there.

In 1493 the Italian explorer Christopher Columbus took chickens on his second expedition to the New World, to provide eggs for the sailors during the voyage. This is how chickens first arrived in the Americas.

▼ These colorful birds live in the jungles of India. Thousands of years ago people began to keep these wild birds for their eggs.

All over the world, chickens are raised for their eggs. This girl from Thailand is tending the family chickens.

In World War II (1939–45) there was a shortage of fresh eggs, and people in Europe had to eat dried or pickled eggs.

During World War II, when there was a shortage of fresh food, many families kept chickens in their backyards.

In World War II, French resistance fighters carried secret messages in eggs. The message was written on the shell using a mixture of alum and vinegar, which was invisible when it dried. When the egg was boiled and peeled, the message could be read on the white inside!

What Is an Egg?

Birds' eggs are laid by female birds; female chickens are called hens. If a female has mated with a male before she lays her eggs, the eggs will be fertilized and a chick may start to grow inside each egg. The hens' eggs we eat have not been fertilized so they do not contain chicks.

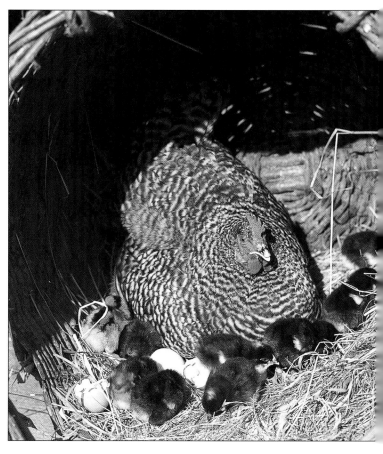

▶ A hen keeps her eggs warm on the nest. Some of her chicks have already hatched and keep close to her for warmth.

▼ A chick hatches out of an egg, using its pointed beak to break the shell.

A chicken's egg has one large and one small end. This makes it roll in a curve, so it will not fall out of a nest. The shell is strong on the outside and helps to prevent other birds or animals from breaking it to eat the chick inside. The shell is weaker on the inside so that the chick can break out when it is ready to hatch.

Hold an egg upright between your finger and thumb and squeeze to see how strong it is. An egg was once dropped from a helicopter 650 feet above the ground and did not break!

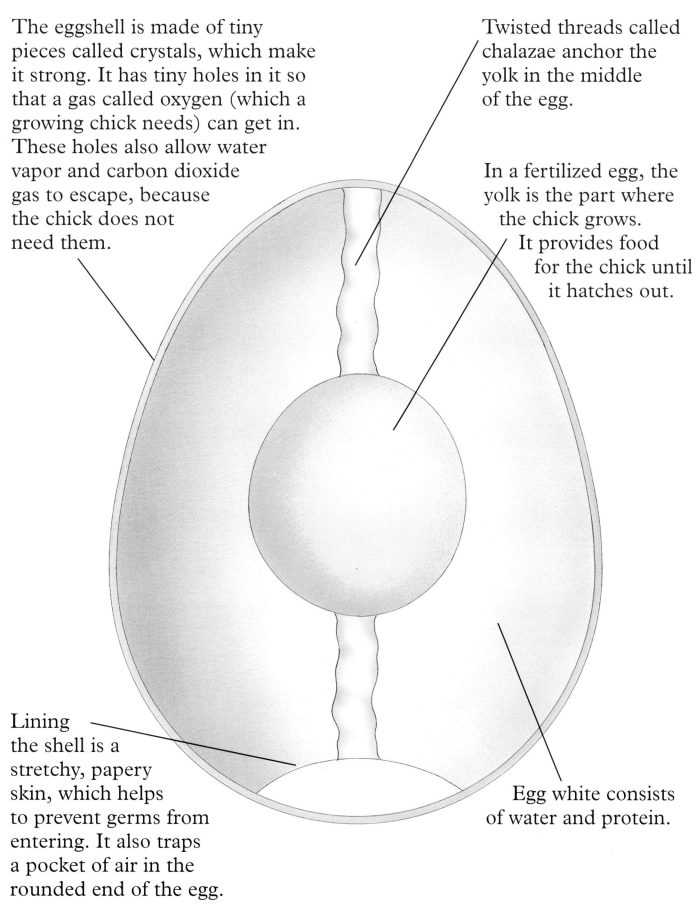

The eggshell is made of tiny pieces called crystals, which make it strong. It has tiny holes in it so that a gas called oxygen (which a growing chick needs) can get in. These holes also allow water vapor and carbon dioxide gas to escape, because the chick does not need them.

Twisted threads called chalazae anchor the yolk in the middle of the egg.

In a fertilized egg, the yolk is the part where the chick grows. It provides food for the chick until it hatches out.

Lining the shell is a stretchy, papery skin, which helps to prevent germs from entering. It also traps a pocket of air in the rounded end of the egg.

Egg white consists of water and protein.

9

The Food in Eggs

Eggs are good for us. They contain protein, which we need to build and repair our bodies. About 10 percent of an egg is protein, which is found in both the yolk and the white. As well as providing protein, eggs help our bodies to take and use proteins from other foods. About 20 percent of an egg is fat, which we need to give us energy. A healthy diet should contain 30 percent fat, or less, and 12 percent protein.

▼ Eggs contain protein, which helps us to grow and stay healthy. They also give us energy.

Eggs also contain vitamins and minerals, mainly in the yolk. They contain Vitamin B_{12}, which is good for the blood and nervous system; Vitamin D, which keeps bones and teeth strong; and Vitamin A, which keeps eyes, skin, and bones healthy. The minerals in eggs include iron, calcium, and iodine. Iron is good for the blood, calcium helps to make strong bones, and iodine helps our bodies to turn food into energy.

▼ Eggs are eaten in most countries of the world. This Chinese girl is eating egg noodles with chopsticks.

Eggs do not contain too many calories, so they are not a fattening food like cakes and cookies. Some food experts believe it is better not to eat eggs every day as they contain some cholesterol and too much cholesterol can harm our hearts. Eggs are still a healthy food and they are easy to digest.

Egg Farming

Egg farmers raise hens that have been bred to lay lots of eggs. They are fed on high-protein foods, which help them to lay plenty of eggs. Some hens can lay between 200 and 300 eggs every year.

Most eggs come from intensive battery farms, where hens are kept in rows of cages in a huge barn. There are three or four hens in each cage and they are never let out. They are fed from troughs and drink from pipes in the cages.

▼ A battery farm in France, where thousands of chickens are kept.

Other farmers keep hens in large barns or deep-litter houses with straw, sand, or wood shavings on the floor. The chickens are kept indoors but they can run around and feed and drink from troughs.

Free-range hens are free to run around outdoors all day, scratching for insects and seeds. The farmer gives them food and water and a hen house to keep them warm and safe at night. Free-range eggs cost more than intensively produced eggs but some people believe battery farming is cruel.

Hens kept outside stop laying in the winter. As a result the farmer loses money. To make the hens think it is spring, battery and deep-litter barns are kept warm and light, so the hens lay eggs all year round.

On all egg farms, the eggs are collected every day. They are stored in a huge refrigerator until they are taken to the packing station.

Free-range chickens like these run around outdoors, looking for food.

In 1974, some free-range hens in the south of France began laying green eggs! The hens had been eating crickets and the color in the insects' bodies was making the eggs green.

The Packing Station

Eggs are taken by trucks from farms to packing stations, where millions of eggs are handled every week. A light shines through the eggs as they pass along a moving belt, to check that the eggs are fresh and have no cracks. Candles were once used for this job, which is still called "candling." Eggs that are not perfect are pasteurized then dried or frozen and used in foods or other products like shampoo, soap, paint, ink, and fertilizer.

Perfect eggs are cleaned and sorted by weight. Five sizes of eggs are sold. The eggs are packed in boxes of one dozen (twelve) or half a dozen, and each box is stamped with the date to show how fresh the eggs are. It takes only a day or two for eggs to get from the farm to the stores and supermarkets where they are sold.

This man, working in an egg factory in Saudi Arabia, is sorting eggs by size.

At a Russian packing station, women pack eggs into boxes.

At home, it is best to store eggs in a refrigerator with the small end down. Eggs should be kept away from strong-smelling foods like fish, as they can take in smells through the tiny holes in their shells. As eggs get older, they lose a little water vapor through these holes and the pocket of air in the rounded end gets bigger. A stale egg weighs less than a fresh egg and will float in water, while a fresh egg will sink. Very stale eggs smell horrible and should not be eaten!

One way of testing the freshness of an egg is to break it open. Fresh eggs have a plump yolk right at the center of the white.

Cooking with Eggs

Eggs can be used in many different ways. They are one of the most useful foods in cooking. A raw egg is runny but sticky. When you beat it and add it to other foods, it helps them to stick together. Fish, meat, or potato cakes can be bound together with egg. If a little egg is brushed on the outside before frying, it gives a crisp coating. Egg also makes breadcrumbs and other coatings stick to foods like fish and chicken.

▼ A selection of sweet and savory dishes made with eggs

This soufflé has puffed up in the oven because air is trapped in the beaten egg whites it contains.

Pancakes are made from a mixture of eggs, flour, and milk. They are cooked on a griddle and can be served with jam, syrup, or a savory filling.

Sometimes cooks separate the yolk from the white for special recipes such as mayonnaise or custard. As an egg yolk cooks the protein hardens, so yolks can be used to thicken sauces and soups. When egg whites are beaten, they become frothy because lots of tiny air bubbles are trapped inside. The protein in the white hardens as it cooks but the air bubbles stay trapped and help foods like meringues, soufflés, and sponge cakes to be light and airy. Egg whites are also used to make ice cream. Lots of foods contain eggs, including cakes, cookies, chocolate pudding, pancakes, egg custards, egg noodles, and fresh pasta.

17

How to Cook Eggs

There are many different ways of cooking eggs. When an egg is raw, the yolk and white are runny. The longer you cook an egg, the firmer it becomes, as the protein sets. Boiling an egg in its shell in water for three minutes gives a soft-boiled egg with runny yolk. Boiling for up to twelve minutes gives a hard-boiled egg. When an egg has been hard boiled, it should be plunged into cold water, which makes it easier to peel and stops the white from turning gray.

▲ A soft-boiled egg with a runny yolk, served with fingers of toast

To poach an egg, break it into a cup and gently tip it into a pan of boiling water and cook for two to three minutes. An egg can also be steamed in a cup that is standing in a pan of boiling water.

Fried eggs are cooked by breaking them into a little hot oil and cooking until they are set.

▶ Frying an egg with the yolk "sunny side up"

An omelette can have lots of different fillings, including cheese, ham, and tomatoes.

To tell if an egg is raw or hard boiled without breaking it, spin it on its pointed end. A raw egg falls over but a hard-boiled egg spins.

To make scrambled eggs or an omelette, the whites and the yolks are beaten together before being cooked in hot oil or butter. Scrambled eggs are stirred during cooking until they are just set. Omelettes are cooked by pouring the beaten egg onto the hot oil or butter and letting the egg spread over the whole pan until it is just firm but not dry. Omelettes are usually folded over, with a filling in the middle. In dishes like Spanish tortilla or Italian frittata, they are cooked like a pancake and then sliced.

To make omelettes or scrambled eggs, you have to break the eggs and beat them with a fork.

Customs and Beliefs

For thousands of years, eggs have been linked with the spring, birth, and new life. Some legends say that the world was created from an egg. A Chinese story tells that the universe was a huge egg until a giant called Pan Gu Lay broke out, scattering the shell, which became the earth, sea, and sky. The Ancient Persians and Egyptians believed that the world hatched from an egg on the first day of spring. They exchanged eggs dyed red or blue to celebrate spring.

The early Christians continued the custom of giving eggs, and this became linked with Easter, the Christian celebration of the rebirth of Christ. Eggs painted or dyed red were said to represent the blood of Christ. Painted eggs were gradually replaced by chocolate eggs, after Spanish explorers brought chocolate to Europe from Mexico in the sixteenth century.

▼ A girl from Hungary decorating an egg for Easter

20

Children hunting for Easter eggs hidden in their yard

In the United States and parts of Europe people hide eggs for children to find on Easter Sunday. Another Easter custom is egg rolling, where everyone joins in rolling eggs down a slope. The last egg to break is said to bring good luck.

At Muslim weddings, wrapped eggs are given to the bride and groom to bring them luck and lots of healthy children. In China, when a baby is born, the family paints eggs red to bring the baby luck.

This egg "tree" was made as a gift for the bride and groom at a Muslim wedding in Malaysia.

Decorating Eggs

Since ancient times, people have decorated eggs to give as gifts in spring and at Easter. There are many ways of decorating eggs. First, they must be hard boiled or blown. A blown (empty) shell lasts much longer. To dye eggs, boil them for about half an hour with a few drops of food coloring or with vegetables—beets for red, onion skins for yellow, cabbage for green. If you draw a design on the shell in lemon juice first, the egg will be colored except where you painted on the lemon. You could make a pattern by sticking flowers or leaves onto the shell before boiling and dyeing the egg.

To blow an egg, use a safety pin to make a hole in the rounded end, then make a slightly bigger hole in the pointed end. Place your fingers over the holes and shake the egg. Holding the egg over a bowl, blow through one end using a straw. When the shell is empty, wash it in cool water with a little dishwashing detergent, then rinse and leave it to dry. You can decorate your blown egg with pens or poster paints, or you can glue on glitter or sequins.

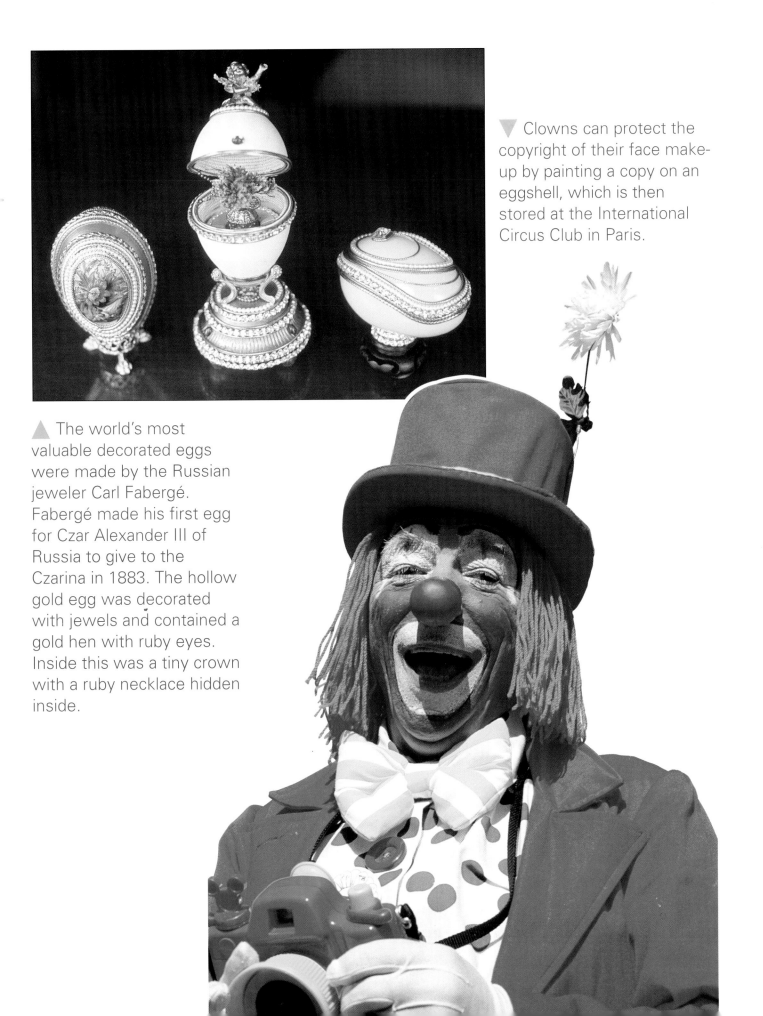

▼ Clowns can protect the copyright of their face make-up by painting a copy on an eggshell, which is then stored at the International Circus Club in Paris.

▲ The world's most valuable decorated eggs were made by the Russian jeweler Carl Fabergé. Fabergé made his first egg for Czar Alexander III of Russia to give to the Czarina in 1883. The hollow gold egg was decorated with jewels and contained a gold hen with ruby eyes. Inside this was a tiny crown with a ruby necklace hidden inside.

Egg Recipes from Around the World

Marbled tea eggs

The Chinese create these decorative eggs by boiling them in spiced tea. The eggs are first hard boiled, then the shells are carefully cracked all over. The eggs are then boiled again in water mixed with black tea, soy sauce, salt, and cinnamon until the whites have become "marbled."

Spanish omelette

An omelette served with a filling of chilis, onions, garlic, tomatoes, olives, capers, and herbs, sprinkled with grated cheese.

English breakfast

The traditional English breakfast consists of fried eggs with bacon, tomatoes, sausages, fried bread, and mushrooms.

Eggs Benedict

A dish made famous by a New York hotel. Poached eggs are served on toast, with a rich sauce made of egg yolks mixed with lemon juice and melted butter.

▲ Chinese marbled eggs look attractive and can be eaten with a salad or for a picnic.

▶ Scotch eggs can be served hot or cold.

Scotch eggs

A favorite picnic dish of hard-boiled eggs coated with sausage meat and breadcrumbs.

Piperade

A dish from the Basque region of France, made from eggs beaten into a mixture of onions, tomatoes, and peppers, cooked in olive oil and garlic.

Chatchouka

A North African dish in which beaten eggs are stirred into a mixture of green peppers, chilis, onions, garlic, and tomatoes.

Egg noodles

Noodles are very popular in the East, where they are eaten with vegetable or meat dishes and in soups. They are a pasta made of fresh eggs and wheat flour, cut into thin strands, and boiled or fried.

Salad Niçoise

This is a cold dish from Nice, in the south of France. It is made with hard-boiled eggs, tuna, anchovies (tiny fish), black olives, green beans, and tomatoes.

▶ A colorful serving of salad Niçoise

Egg Recipes for You to Try

Greek-style scrambled eggs

To serve each person you will need:

2 eggs
1 tablespoon olive oil
1-3/4 ounces Greek feta cheese, crumbled
a pinch of chopped fresh or dried herbs
a pinch of salt and pepper

1 Using a fork, beat the eggs together in a bowl with a pinch of salt and pepper and the herbs.

2 Ask an adult to help you to heat the oil in a frying pan.

3 Pour in the egg mixture. Keep stirring the eggs with a fork until they begin to set.

4 Take the pan off the heat before the eggs become dry and rubbery. Sprinkle the crumbled feta cheese over the top.

Serve with crusty bread and a salad.

Lemon omelette soufflé

To serve two people you will need:

3 large eggs, with the yolks
 and whites separated
2 tablespoons sugar
juice of one lemon
grated rind of one lemon
1-1/2 tablespoons butter

1 Tap each egg firmly but carefully on the side of a bowl to break the shell in two. Holding the egg over the bowl, slide the yolk from one half of the shell to the other, letting the white run out into the bowl. Put the yolks into a separate bowl and beat them up with a fork.

2 Add the sugar, lemon rind, and juice to the egg yolks and mix well until they are thick and smooth.

3 In another bowl, beat the egg whites using an egg whisk until they are quite stiff and you can make them stand up in little peaks.

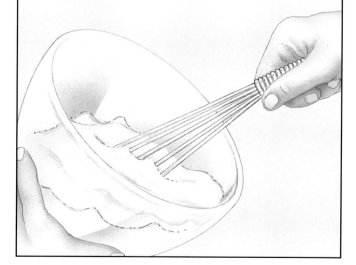

28

4 Fold the whites carefully into the yolk mixture. Don't beat or stir too hard as you don't want to burst the air bubbles!

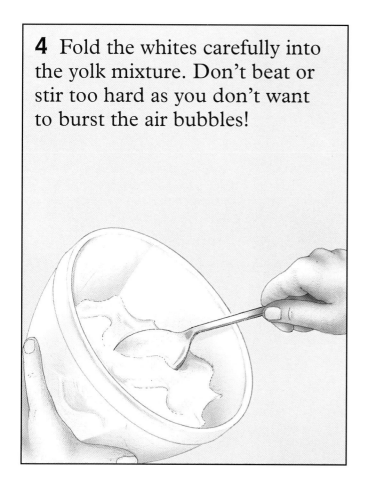

5 Ask an adult to help you to melt the butter in a frying pan. When it starts to froth, pour in the egg mixture. Tilt the pan from side to side and use a spatula to lift the edges to help cook the omelette.

6 When the omelette has just set, take the pan off the heat and put it under the broiler for a minute or two to give a crisp brown topping.

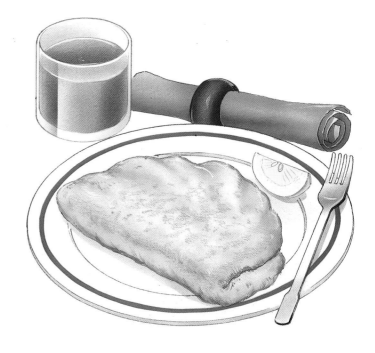

Fold the omelette in two and serve quickly.

Glossary

alum   A substance made from the metal aluminum.

Ancient Greek   From the period in Greek History of about 1000–400 B.C.

Ancient Roman   From the period in Roman history of about 753 B.C.–410 A.D.

battery farming   A way of farming large numbers of animals to increase production and reduce costs.

calories   A measurement of the energy in food.

candling   The system of shining a light through an egg to check whether it is fresh and undamaged.

capers   Flower buds or young berries of the caper plant.

cholesterol   A substance found in our bodies and in some foods that may cause heart disease.

copyright   The legal right to be the only producer or publisher of something.

crystals   Tiny parts that make up many solids, including eggshell.

deep-litter farming   A farming method where poultry is kept in barns with a thick layer of straw, sand, or wood shavings on the floor, to absorb droppings.

dressing   A sauce for food.

fertilized   Able to produce young. A fertilized egg is laid by a female bird that has mated with a male.

fossilized   Hardened in rock, usually after many years.

free-range farming   A way of keeping poultry that allows them to roam free, looking for food.

intensive farming   A type of farming that aims to produce large amounts of product at the lowest possible cost.

medieval   From the period of the Middle Ages, about A.D. 500 to 1500.

minerals   Substances formed in the earth and found in food, which we need to keep our bodies healthy.

nervous system   The network of nerves in the body that allow us to hear, smell, see, touch, and taste.

packing station   The place where eggs are sorted and packed.

pasteurized   Sterilized, or made free of germs.

protein   A substance found in food that we need to grow and repair our bodies.

resistance fighters   People who worked against the occupation of France by Germany during World War II (1939–45).

saltpeter   A salty mineral.

spatula A wide, flat spoon for stirring, spreading, and mixing.

vitamins Substances found in food that we need to keep us healthy.

water vapor Tiny droplets of water in the air.

Books to Read

Food and Feasts series. New York: New Discovery. Historical glances at how various cultures ate the food they did and why these particular foods were eaten by the civilization.

Food Around the World series. New York: Thomson Learning. A series of ten books on food by country. Each book presents the particular ways in which the peoples of different countries prepare and serve their food. Simple recipes are also provided.

Dibble, Lisa. *Food and Farming*. New York: Dorling Kindersley, 1993.

Jones, Norma. *Food: What Do We Eat and Where Does It Come From*. Wylie, TX: Info Plus TX, 1992.

Kowtaluk, Hellen. *Discovering Food*. Peoria, IL: Bennet IL, 1982.

Moss, Miriam. *Eat Well*. New York: Macmillan Children's Group, 1993.

Perl, Lila. *Junk Food, Fast Food, Health Food: What America Eats and Why*. New York: Houghton Mifflin, 1980.

Tames, Richard. *Food: Feasts, Cooks, and Kitchens*. New York: Franklin Watts, 1994.

Index

Numbers in **bold** show subjects that appear in pictures.